HOPE IN A TIME OF CHANGE

A Course for Lent 1998

CCBI
Inter-Church House
35-41 Lower Marsh
London SE1 7RL

ISBN 0 85169 240 0

© 1997 Council of Churches for Britain and Ireland

CCBI
Inter-Church House
35-41 Lower Marsh
London SE1 7RL

Design and typesetting by Mark Whitchurch Art & Design

Printed by Ebenezer Baylis & Son,
The Trinity Press, London Road, Worcester

Contents

Preface by CCBI Presidents	2
Introduction	3
Notes for Participants	6
Notes for Leaders	7
Session One *Hope Through Change*	10
Session Two *Hope Through Discipline*	18
Session Three *Hope Through Christ*	24
Session Four *Hope Through Tears*	29
Session Five *Hope Through Vision*	38
Useful Addresses	43
Members of the Lent 1998 Planning Group	44
Evaluation	45

Aim of the course:
This course is intended to help Christians to reflect on hope as the Millennium approaches.

Preface

Over the past few years Christians have been meeting in local ecumenical groups during Lent to share different aspects of their **faith** and the ways in which their **love** is expressed through concern for justice and for reconciliation. In Lent 1998 they are invited to share with one another their Christian **hope** at a time when the advent of the third Christian Millennium heightens our awareness of change in the world and in the church.

As Presidents of the Council of Churches for Britain and Ireland we warmly commend this biblically-based 1998 Lent Course to our member churches; we urge them to promote its use by local congregations, wherever possible in an ecumenical context. We have an opportunity to encourage and to learn from one another as together we explore the theme of **hope.**

In the wider context of the world church, local ecumenical groups in Lent 1998 are also invited to contribute to preparation within Britain and Ireland for the eighth World Council of Churches Assembly in Harare, Zimbabwe, in December 1998 on the theme 'Turn to God: Rejoice in Hope' by sharing what they have experienced with the churches' delegates to that Assembly.

We are grateful to the Lent 1998 Planning Group for its work which CCBI is sponsoring in association with the national ecumenical bodies.

Rev Hugh Davidson	Mrs Gillian Kingston	Rt Rev Alwyn Rice Jones
Rev Io Smith	Rev David Staple	Cardinal Thomas Winning

Presidents of the Council of Churches for Britain and Ireland

Introduction

Hope in a Time of Change

Hope in a Time of Change is a course for Lent and has been written to emphasise the Christian virtue of hope as it is presented in the Bible. Hope may sometimes seem to be in short supply but it remains one of the key Christian virtues and one of the most important gifts that we can bring into our life in the world. As we approach the end of the Millennium many people will be thinking about the future; some even believe that there is no future. As Christians we are challenged to be people of hope, and to do all that we can to see hopes fulfilled. Because of the hope that we have through belief in Christ, hope is one of the gifts that the Church should be able to offer to those who have least hope. And because the hope that Christ offered was hope for the present life as well as the future, the hope that we can offer might be shown in our lives and in the way that we treat those who share this world with us.

Thinking about the Third Millennium

One of the proposals for how Christians should mark the coming of the Third Millennium includes a programme of preparation. Pope John Paul II has suggested that in each of the three years before 2000 AD we might focus on certain key themes based on the persons of the Trinity.

1997 was the suggested year for reflecting on the person of Jesus and considering the Christian virtue of faith.

1998 is proposed as a year of focussing on the Holy Spirit, on renewal of hope and on the value of unity.

1999 would direct our attention to the person of God the Father, reconciliation, the virtue of charity, and the remission of debt.

Christian churches see the year 2000 as significant in relation to what they believe about Jesus Christ: it is not merely a change of date, but a moment to focus on the activity of God in history, revealed to us in Christ. So Christians share with others in our culture the emotional resonance of reaching this date, and the future which lies beyond it, but more fundamentally they see it as an invitation to renewal in faith and commitment to God's mission. So Christians, like others, see the Millennium as a chance to do some thinking about where we have come from and what the future may hold, and how we want to shape it. The idea of sorting out some of the injustices imposed by humanity upon humanity has been given fresh impetus as many people agree that we should try to leave the evils of the past behind and enter the next 1000 years with a fresh start. Indeed many Christians from different churches have been encouraged by the Pope's call for a year of Jubilee in 2000. This would involve action in relation to the option for the poor and the remission of debt.

Hope Changes the World
Churches in Britain and Ireland have already begun their planning for the year 2000. A sample of some of these plans shows how *Hope in a Time of Change* reflects many of the themes and objectives being considered by the churches at this time.
Action of Churches Together in Scotland (ACTS) has already begun a four-year programme of preparation for the year 2000 with 1998 being the Year of Hope.
In Wales an action group has been formed to work on 'debt in Wales' as part of the churches' preparation for the new Millennium. Churches Together in England has published a booklet on marking the Millennium called *A Chance to Start Again*. This presents some ideas about how the Churches might respond to the year 2000 and beyond. The power of Christian hope is summarised in this way:
"Christians believe that Jesus Christ and the Christian way of looking at things can lead to:
- people finding meaning in a bewildering world
- people finding hope as they face the uncertainties of the future
- people finding the motivation to do something about changing the world.

By calling to mind the story of Christ, and the many positive components within our Christian heritage, there are visions to be caught about the future."

Hope in a Time of Change aims to encourage many people to take a fresh look at the Bible, to explore the visions of hope presented in scripture, and to be renewed in our own vision, and strengthened in preparation for whatever action may be needed to ensure that the Reign of God will be more visible in the Third Millennium of the Christian Faith.

Partners in Learning
Hope in a Time of Change has been developed and written in connection with *Partners in Learning*. *Partners in Learning* is an ecumenical publication that provides all-age worship and learning resources for churches throughout the year
The *Partners in Learning* material has been designed to complement the Lent course, and draw a link between what is done in Lent groups and Sunday worship and learning. This is the first time this link has been made, and we hope that it will enrich people's experience. if you would like more information about *Partners in Learning*, and how to obtain a copy of these materials please contact the CCBI Bookroom, or write to *Partners in Learning* Distribution, 1020 Bristol Road, Selly Oak, Birmingham B29 6LB.

Other initiatives in 1998
Hope in a Time of Change is a course that has been planned to relate to some of the other initiatives that will be part of the life of the Church in 1998.
The reports from groups and individuals about their experiences of doing the course will be used to help the representatives from Britain and Ireland who will going to the 1998 Assembly of the World Council of Churches, Harare, on the theme, "Turn to God: Rejoice in Hope".
1998 is also the final year of the Decade of Churches in Solidarity with Women. We hope that many groups will want to adapt the materials to consider some of the themes of this Decade and to reflect on what has been achieved through the Decade.
A major initiative in England will be The Open Book project which aims to organise events throughout the country to reflect the

special focus on the Bible that is one of the themes for Millennium preparation in this year. The 1998 Lent Course is one way by which the churches in England can be part of The Open Book project, 'opening the Bible to the people – and the people to the Bible'.

Addresses for further information about the Decade of Churches in Solidarity with Women and about The Open Book can be found at the back of this course book on page 43.

Notes for Participants
Who needs to have a copy of the course book?
We hope that everyone who does the course will want to have their own copy of the course book so that they can have a sense of how the course will develop and also read the background information for each session and use the scripture passages for personal reflection. Further copies of this book can be ordered from the CCBI Bookroom, Inter-Church House, 35-41 Lower Marsh, London SE1 7RL.

What version of the Bible was used to prepare this course?
The excerpts from the Bible used in this course are taken from the New Revised Standard Version published by the Oxford University Press.

What should we do with the boxed texts
There are two types of boxed text.

> The Bible passages which are the very core of this Lent course are highlighted by being enclosed by a double border like the one around this paragraph.

> A single line border like the one around this paragraph highlights additional resources or background information that some groups might like to use. The background

> information will be especially useful for those who want to look at the Bible passages in greater depth – either in group discussion or for study at home after the session.

Notes for Leaders

Hope in a Time of Change is the Lent course for 1998 prepared by the Council of Churches for Britain and Ireland (CCBI). The course is offered throughout Britain and Ireland in the same way as previous courses like *Building Bridges* (1996) and *Have Another Look* (1994).

As a group leader you may find that this course needs more preparation than was needed for courses in previous years. You will need to read through each session in advance, looking at which sections might work best in your group. You may also find it helpful to read through the whole course beforehand. This will give you an idea of how the five sessions are linked. As you do this you might like to keep in mind that the course is designed to explore the idea of hope as it is found in the Bible. This could well be the first time that some people in your group will have looked at Biblical texts in detail. Some groups will want to approach the Bible passages in different ways, using some of the approaches that have been developed by scripture scholars. If you already know the people who will be in your group then you might be able to imagine how the discussions will develop and choose sections from the sessions that will help the discussion along. If you don't know the people who will be in your group then you might want to spend some time in the first session talking about what people expect from the course.

Some of the exercises and topics in this course may bring up painful memories for some of the participants. Before beginning the course it would, therefore, be good to ask people to treat the discussions as confidential. You might also want to have the name of a minister or counsellor to whom people could talk if they felt it necessary.

Who could be involved?
Anyone who is interested! The ideal group should have members from different traditions so that the various viewpoints will lead to better discussion and an improved understanding. Some people will be regular church goers while others might not.

How many in a group?
If there are too few the group finds it hard to get going; too many and it becomes impersonal. For this course six to ten might be best.

How often should the group meet?
Hope in a time of Change is designed for five weekly meetings in Lent.

How long should each session last?
The sessions are designed to last for about 90 minutes. Some people will prefer to reduce this time to 75 minutes. The actual length should be decided by the group leader having considered the needs of the group.

Based on 90 minutes the typical session might look like this:
Welcome and opening prayer:	5 minutes
Starting point and discussion of theme:	25 minutes
Reading of Bible text and discussion:	45 minutes
Preparation for next session:	5 minutes
Closing worship:	10 minutes

The length of time needed for some of the parts in the five sessions will vary; e.g. you will need longer for the welcome and introductions in the first session and some time towards the end of the fifth session for the evaluation. But on the whole each session should take no more than 90 minutes. Because some parts of the course will need slightly less or more time we have indicated in the text the time that each part might take.

How should we talk about the Bible?
If your group is drawn from different traditions you may be surprised at the range of different experiences of reading the Bible. Some will read the Bible every day, some will come from

churches where decisions are clearly based on passages from scripture, some will have made a special study of the Bible and be familiar with different approaches to reading scripture, while others might not have read the Bible for themselves.

It is important that everyone is able to participate in the discussions so leaders might have to encourage people to avoid using 'jargon' words. Sometimes it might be helpful if participants explain what they mean so that people from other traditions can relate these to different ideas used in their own churches or groups.

The sessions in this course represent different approaches to Bible study. The planning group included people from different traditions.

Course Prayer

You might like to use the following prayer as the opening prayer for each of the five sessions:

> *God our Hope,*
> *You draw us ever onwards*
> *Towards the time of our salvation.*
> *May your Spirit free us from fear of change*
> *And nurture in us the joys of expectation,*
> *That we may be ready to grasp the future,*
> *So that our hope in you*
> *May become the hope of the world.*
> *In the name of Jesus Christ. Amen.*

Acknowledgements

Permission to reproduce the following copyright materials has been given by the publishers/authors or applied for:

Richard Foster, *Freedom of Simplicity*, Triangle/SPCK, London 1981.

Frances Young, *Face to Face: A narrative essay in the theology of suffering*, T&T Clark, Edinburgh 1990.

The Scripture quotations contained herein are from the New Revised Standard Version of the Bible, Anglicized Edition, copyright ©1989, 1995 by the Division of Christian Education of the National Council of the Churches of Christ in the United States of America, and are used by permission. All rights reserved.

Session 1

Hope Through Change

Aim
To introduce the overall theme and to explore the concept and relevance of Jubilee.

Welcome and Opening Prayer   15 minutes
The group leader welcomes participants to this the first session of the course and the session is opened with a short prayer (a suggested prayer for the course can be found on page 9). Participants introduce themselves to the group and say why they have come.

Starting Point   30 minutes
Times of Change

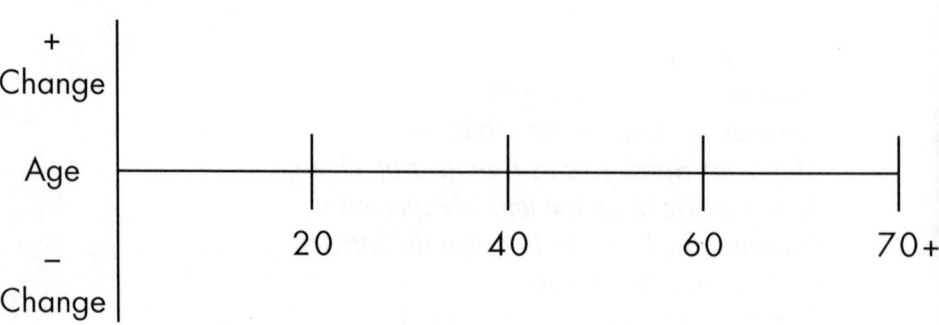

On your own
On the time line above mark in some significant times of change or challenge in your life. If you view these times of change as positive place them above the horizontal line. If you view them as negative place them below the line.

Try and recall some of your feelings at the time e.g. excitement, apprehension, anticipation, disappointment.

What hopes were fulfilled or dashed?

In pairs or in the group
Share one of your significant times of change and how this time was linked to hope or the lack of hope.

The group should read the following:
Memory and Hope in Times of Change
Many of our conversations begin with the words "I remember when … " In the flow of recalling an event or experience we can touch deep pain, erupt in laughter, sigh in despair, overflow with excitement, raise our hands in gratitude or be renewed in hope.

Memory acts as the storehouse of our thoughts, words, feelings and experiences of events and relationships lived by us as individuals or as a group in the past. Our individual memories and collective memories interweave to inform our present and shape our future. Our memories can be subversive, comforting, terrifying or reviving.

Perhaps one of the functions of memory is to serve hope. We speak of hope as being an anchor, a refuge, and a lifeline on which we depend. We might also think of hope as an essential Christian virtue. It is an attitude of the heart and involves an orientation towards the future in the light of the promises given in the past and trusted in while journeying in the present.

At special times in life we see how memory serves hope. These special moments such as anniversaries, and jubilees can lead us to an appreciation of who we are and from where we have come. They can also engage us in a reappraisal and reorientation of our lives. They enable us to locate sources of hope for the way ahead.

Jubilee 'Moments'

In the Group
Recall any memories of jubilee celebrations or special anniversaries in which you have participated.

How was the jubilee celebrated?

Were there any special gifts exchanged, symbols used?

How did the memory of the past and hopes for the future meet in the moment of jubilee?

Jubilee and Hope
Jubilee is linked in a deep way to memory and hope. The past is recalled in order to celebrate the present and give direction and hope to the future. The Hebrew word that Jubilee comes from is Yobel which means "trumpet blast". The Jubilee year was to be proclaimed on Yom Kippur (Day of Atonement), the most sacred day of the year. The trumpet blast of the horn was given added significance in the fiftieth year, the year of Jubilee. This day proclaimed not only a release of the community from the guilt of sin for another year but also a year of rest, release from debt, return to the land and the hope of renewing relationship with God, others and the environment.

Bible Reading and Discussion 30 minutes

Leviticus 25:8-19, 23

⁸ You shall count off seven weeks of years, seven times seven years, so that the period of seven weeks of years gives forty nine years. ⁹ Then you shall have the trumpet sounded loud; on the tenth day of the seventh month - on the day of atonement - you shall have the trumpet sounded throughout all your land. ¹⁰ And you shall

hallow the fiftieth year and you shall proclaim liberty throughout the land to all its inhabitants. It shall be a jubilee for you: you shall return, every one of you, to your property and every one of you to your family. 11 *That fiftieth year shall be a jubilee for you: you shall not sow, or reap the aftergrowth, or harvest the unpruned vines.* 12 *For it is a jubilee; it shall be holy to you: you shall eat only what the field itself produces.*
13 *In this year of jubilee you shall return, every one of you, to your property.* 14 *When you make a sale to your neighbour or buy from your neighbour, you shall not cheat one another.* 15 *When you buy from your neighbour, you shall pay only for the number of years since the jubilee; the seller shall charge you only for the remaining crop-years.* 16 *If the years are more, you shall increase the price, and if the years are fewer, you shall diminish the price; for it is a certain number of harvests that are being sold to you.* 17 *You shall not cheat one another, but you shall fear your God; for I am the Lord your God.*
18 *You shall observe my statutes and faithfully keep my ordinances, so that you may live on the land securely.* 19 *The land will yield its fruit, and you will eat your fill and live on it securely.* ... 23 *The land shall not be sold in perpetuity, for the land is mine; with me you are but aliens and tenants.*

Jubilee as a Source of Hope
In twos or threes
What does the passage say about the
- relationship of people to the land?
- relationship of people to each other?
- relationship of people to God?

Share your findings with the larger group.

Imagine you are a peasant farmer or small shop keeper facing bankruptcy. What hope would Jubilee give you?

If you had the opportunity to start something in our world all over again what would you like to begin? What might prevent you?

Think of what our Christian faith says about starting all over again. In what ways can this be a source of hope for the world?

Preparation for next session   5 minutes
It would be helpful if participants can think about different types of fasting before the next session. Try not to get into a discussion of this now.

You might think about slimming, fasting in order to improve our body-image. Why do we do this? What do we think about the "slimming industry"? What about anorexia and other serious eating disorders?

You might think about fasting with a very particular object in mind, for instance joining a sponsored fast such as those organised by Cafod and SCIAF each year or the frugal meals organised by Christian Aid.

If you have no experience in the group of the religious fast, are you aware of Jewish neighbours fasting for Yom Kippur or Muslims fasting for Ramadan? What do we do it for?

Worship  10 minutes
In this session we have been looking at the idea of Jubilee and the call to change. Let's listen now to Jesus: what is he saying to us in *our* Lent?

Mark 1:12-15

Please read very slowly:
¹² *And the Spirit immediately drove him out into the wilderness.* ¹³ *He was in the wilderness for forty days, tempted by Satan; and he was with the wild beasts; and the angels waited on him.* ¹⁴ *Now after John was arrested, Jesus came to Galilee, proclaiming the good news of God,* ¹⁵ *and saying, 'The time is fulfilled,* (pause) *and the kingdom of God has come near;* (pause) *repent,* (pause) *and believe in the good news.'* (pause)

Group members may wish to voice their own hopes for the course.

Concluding Prayer
Say together:

We pray for Hope; hope for ourselves, hope for our families, friends, colleagues, and hope for the world.
We pray that our hope will free us to be people of justice, companions of the oppressed, and active builders of the reign of God's hope. Lord, guide us through this Lenten season, as we prepare for your resurrection in hope and glory. Amen

Additional Resources for Session One

Background to Jubilee
According to the opening words of the chapter, these words were spoken by the Lord to Moses on Mount Sinai as instructions to the Israelites on how they were to live their life in the land he was bringing them to. Usually we call this kind of writing 'law' but it is not quite what we mean by law in modern secular life. It sets out an ideal for the nation's life but it does not suggest how it is to be enforced in practice. There is no human penalty for disobedience, only God's wrath. *(Leviticus 26)*
Some readers would literally believe in the setting given in v.1. Others would regard this and other laws of the Old Testament as the work of later writers who responded to problems in the life of the nation with solutions that they believed to be of God and therefore included in the account of his dealings with his people at the beginning.

To understand the law, we need to understand the practicalities of life in ancient Israel:
- Most people were peasants working the land and supplying most of their needs themselves.

- Land was held in families and passed down from father to son.
- The male head of the family for the time being was regarded as the landowner
- The family depended on their land for their livelihood, but they or their head also relied on it for their standing in the community.
- The land was thought of as a family or tribal possession which an individual could not deal with as he liked (see 1Kings 21:3)

No one then would willingly give up their land. But they might be forced to. Agriculture was risky, and after a bad harvest a man might have to borrow corn or money. If he was unable to repay, he risked losing whatever he had put up for security. This could be a child, who would have to serve as an indentured servant, or even be sold into permanent slavery. If bad times continued he might have to sell 'his' land. Without land, he might become a slave or a labourer hiring himself out by day or at best a tenant on the land that was his ancestors'. He lost all standing in his community, and might have to move far away, perhaps drift to the big city.

There was no lack of wealthy people, officials or merchants or well-to-do farmers, who were ready to buy up land or foreclose on mortgages. For them, land was simply a commodity. They are denounced by the prophets: see Isaiah 5:8 or Micah 2: 1-2.

This law establishes a theological principle (v23) which would deny anyone absolute rights over the land. It tries to set up a system for enabling people

- to start over again,
- to return to their land (or more likely their father's),
- to be released from slavery,
- to be rescued from poverty,
- to renew shattered communities.

Jubilee – Hope for the Millennium
Jubilee looks to a time of change, to a return to a right order, a 'favourable year of the Lord'. Another way of expressing this is the coming of the Kingdom of God (Mark 1:12-15). The kingdom (or 'reign') of God is expressed in two time dimensions – the rule of God in the 'now' and awaiting in joyful hope of the 'not yet'.

Jubilee hope is linked to the prospect that those deprived of wealth, alienated from the land, from their own labour and from each other will be able to experience a deliverance from the backlog of unpayable debt, a liberation from oppression and injustice.

The Jubilee 2000 Campaign
The Jubilee 2000 campaign seeks to give expression to such a vision. It seeks in particular to remit the inert debt which has been built up from the exceptional years of the oil decade, 1973 - 1983, when loans were pressed on the governments of the South, in the fallacious assumption they would be wisely used, rates of interest would remain low – and terms of trade remain favourable for developing countries.
The campaign models itself on the 18th century campaign to abolish slavery. That was led in Britain by men and women in the Church, responding to the leadership and resistance of slaves on plantations, and linking up with others across the world.
To join Jubilee 2000 send a cheque/postal order, made payable to Jubilee 2000 Campaign, for £16 (£8 unwaged) for one year's membership to: Celia Willoughby, Administrator, Jubilee 2000, PO Box 100, London SE1 7RT.
Further information about the campaign is also available from this address.

Session 2

Hope Through Discipline

Aim
To explore the place of discipline in the Christian Life.

Welcome and Opening Prayer　　　　　　5 minutes

Starting Point　　　　　　　　　　　　25 minutes
Fasting was very important in the Judaism in which Jesus grew up. Fasting was also important in the early church, and retains a special importance in Orthodox and Roman Catholic tradition, in Pentecostal and Independent churches, in charismatic movements, and in many other churches around the world.

Feedback from preparation done at the end of last week's session
What part does fasting play in your life?
And in the life of your church?

What special disciplines are part of your church's life?
e.g.　Sunday observance, use of alcohol, smoking, dress, Lent, Advent, before Communion.
　　　Even if we don't fast, are there other observances our churches expect us to keep?

Discuss what you think of the following passage:

**Some thoughts on fasting
from Richard Foster's *Freedom of Simplicity***

"Fasting helps to give us balance. It makes us more keenly sensitive to the whole of life, so that we do not become obsessed with our consumer mentality. It is something of an inner alarm to help us hold our priorities straight, to give us a sense of spiritual sensitivity."

"Fasting reveals the things that control us. We cover up what is inside us with food and good things, but in fasting these things come to the surface. The first truth that was revealed to me in my early experiences in fasting was my lust for good feelings. It is certainly not a bad thing to feel good, but we must be able to bring that feeling to an easy place where it does not control us. So many attitudes strive to control us: anger, pride, fear, hostility, gluttony, avarice. All of these and more will surface as we fast. it is a blessed release to have these things out in the open so they can be defeated, and we can live with a single eye toward God."

Richard Foster goes on to suggest fasting from people (i.e. by spending time in solitude), from the media, and from the telephone.

Richard Foster, *Freedom of Simplicity*, Triangle/SPCK, London 1981, p. 138.

Bible Reading and Discussion 45 minutes
Setting the Scene
The next paragraph helps to put the Isaiah text in context. Read this before moving on to the passage from the prophet.

In the last part of the Book of Isaiah, the prophet is speaking to a nation that is just being rebuilt, economically, socially and spiritually, on return from exile in Babylon. There is great hope and exhilaration and a new spirit of openness; but there are temptations, too – to corruption in trade and a lack of care for vulnerable people, to losing hold on the faith that has sustained the exiles in favour of the Canaanite religious practices of the homeland, to religious exclusivism. As with last week's passage, we begin with a trumpet-call. Read the passage aloud, enjoying its poetry and power while listening for its answer to the question "What is a true fast?".
You might like to read the following passage aloud, using four different voices (A, B, C, and D) as indicated.

Isaiah 58: 1–12

A ¹ *Shout out, do not hold back!*
    Lift up your voice like a trumpet!
B *Announce to my people their rebellion,*
    to the house of Jacob their sins.
C ² *Yet day after day they seek me and delight to know my ways,*
    as if they were a nation that practised righteousness
    and did not forsake the ordinance of their God;
    they ask of me righteous judgments,
    they delight to draw near to God.
D ³ *"Why do we fast, but you do not see?*
    Why humble ourselves, but you do not notice?"
A *Look, you serve your own interest on your fast day,*
    and oppress all your workers.
B ⁴ *Look, you fast only to quarrel and to fight*
    and to strike with a wicked fist.
C *Such fasting as you do today*
    will not make your voice heard on high.
D ⁵ *Is such the fast that I choose, a day to humble oneself?*
    Is it to bow down the head like a bulrush,
    and to lie in sackcloth and ashes?
    Will you call this a fast, a day acceptable to the Lord?
A ⁶ *Is not this the fast that I choose:*
    to loose the bonds of injustice,
    to undo the thongs of the yoke,
    to let the oppressed go free,
    and to break every yoke?
B ⁷ *Is it not to share your bread with the hungry,*
    and bring the homeless poor into your house;
    when you see the naked, to cover them,
    and not to hide yourself from your own kin?
C ⁸ *Then your light shall break forth like the dawn,*
    and your healing shall spring up quickly;
    your vindicator shall go before you,

> *the glory of the Lord shall be your rear guard.*
> D *⁹Then you shall call, and the Lord will answer;*
> *you shall cry for help, and he will say, Here I am.*
> A *If you remove the yoke from among you,*
> *the pointing of the finger, the speaking of evil,*
> *¹⁰ if you offer your food to the hungry*
> *and satisfy the needs of the afflicted,*
> *then your light shall rise in the darkness*
> *and your gloom be like the noonday.*
> B *¹¹ The Lord will guide you continually,*
> *and satisfy your needs in parched places,*
> *and make your bones strong;*
> *and you shall be like a watered garden,*
> *like a spring of water, whose waters never fail.*
> C *¹² Your ancient ruins shall be rebuilt;*
> *you shall raise up the foundations of many generations;*
> *you shall be called the repairer of the breach,*
> *the restorer of streets to live in.*

Has the passage told you anything about fasting that you hadn't already discussed?
Focusing especially on verses 6-7, what would you now say is a 'fast' for:
- Individuals today?
- Christian communities today?

How would such 'fasting' change your priorities? Your church's? What kind of impact would it have on your local neighbourhood? – on the nation? – on the world?
– What kind of 'fasting' do you think the prophet would be recommending for Christians now, in the West, as we look forward to the Millennium?

Exercise
Write, together, your own version of Isaiah 58:5-7.
Begin "Is such the fast that I choose"(Isaiah 58:5) and list the things you would now identify as "false fasting".

Continue with "Is this not the fast that I choose" (Isaiah 58:6) and list the things you think are "true fasting".
Use this in your concluding worship.

Preparation for the next session 5 minutes

The next session begins with memories of childhood. You might like to spend a few minutes in the next few days thinking about a particular memory to share. Group members could bring along a photograph or special object from their childhood.

Worship  10 minutes

In this session we have been looking at fasting. Read through the version of Isaiah 58:5-7 that your group has written. Jesus challenges our views: through him hope is fulfilled, but here we are, his followers, still longing for fulfilment.

Mark 2: 18-22

[18] Now John's disciples and the Pharisees were fasting; and people came and said to him,
"Why do John's disciples and the disciples of the Pharisees fast, but your disciples do not fast?"
[19] Jesus said to them,
"The wedding guests cannot fast while the bridegroom is with them, can they? As long as they have the bridegroom with them, they cannot fast.
[20] The days will come when the bridegroom is taken away from them, and then they will fast on that day.
[21] No-one sews a piece of unshrunk cloth on to an old cloak; otherwise, the patch pulls away from it, the new from the old, and a worse tear is made.
[22] And no-one puts new wine into old wine-skins, otherwise, the wine will burst the skins, and the wine is lost, and so are the skins; but one puts new wine into fresh wineskins".

Concluding Prayer
Say together:

Lord Jesus Christ
You are the bridegroom at the feast;
you are the new wine and the new life;
yet we are still unfulfilled.
We ask that the discipline we undertake
may prepare us to enjoy your presence,
and may loose the bonds of injustice,
relieve the weight of oppression,
bring food to the hungry,
and meet the needs of the afflicted.
We ask this so that
our light may break forth like the dawn,
and our healing spring up quickly,
this Lent,
this beginning of the new Millennium,
and in the years that lie ahead.
Amen.

Session 3

Hope Through Christ

Aim
To explore how our doubts and fears are met through our hope in Jesus as Messiah.

Welcome and Opening Prayer　　　　　5 minutes

Starting Point　　　　　　　　　　　20 minutes
Share in pairs any childhood memories relating to fear and doubts, (for example, constantly turning on the light during the night to make sure that the light had not disappeared).

Together discuss how we addressed these fears. If we succeeded in overcoming our fears and doubts what influences guided and helped us?
- As individuals, what fears and doubts do we ever have before committing ourselves to a new experience.
- What doubts do we hear expressed about the future within the communities we live in?
- How do we deal with these doubts?

'Doubt is not always a sign that a man is wrong', said Oswald Chambers, 'it may be a sign that he is thinking.' We can look back at the ministry of Jesus, and understand what he was doing; John the Baptist did not have that advantage.

Bible reading and discussion 　　50 minutes

Luke 7:18-23

[18] *The disciples of John reported all these things to him. So John summoned two of his disciples* [19] *and sent them to the Lord to ask, 'Are you the one who is to come, or are we to wait for another?'* [20] *When the*

men had come to him, they said, 'John the Baptist has sent us to you to ask, "Are you the one who is to come, or are we to wait for another?"' ²¹ Jesus had just then cured many people of diseases, plagues, and evil spirits, and had given sight to many who were blind. ²² And he answered them, 'Go and tell John what you have seen and heard: the blind receive their sight, the lame walk, the lepers are cleansed, the deaf hear, the dead are raised, the poor have good news brought to them. ²³ And blessed is anyone who takes no offence at me.'

Background to Luke 7:18-23

What does John mean by 'the one who is to come'? The Gospel of Luke itself offers a clear answer. In 3:16-17 John the Baptist had prophesied the coming of one mightier than himself who would 'baptize you with the Holy Spirit and fire' and 'clear his threshing-floor' – acts of judgement and power. This expectation had not been obviously fulfilled in Jesus' career to date. But Jesus in his answer points John to Jesus' own manifesto in 4:18-21, where he takes as his programme the speech in Isaiah 61:1-2, placed by the prophet in the mouth of a kingly figure whose first concern is good news for the poor and powerless.

Both John's expectation and Jesus' programme, or the way Luke presents them, may be linked with hopes current among many Jews at the time for an end to the present oppressive structures of power, whether under the Romans or native rulers like Herod Antipas. They looked for God to reverse the situation, and some of them expected a ruler to emerge of the line of David who would act to clear the Holy Land of oppressors and rule in justice. There were many varieties of belief; we cannot generalise. Probably only some Jews talked about a Messiah, *the* 'one who is to come'. But Christians came to believe that Jesus was Messiah, so the Gospels emphasise this concept. Luke had to show that it

> made sense to claim this for Jesus, whose earthly career lacked political power. He does this by highlighting Isaiah 61 as Jesus' programme and linking it with Jesus' option for the poor in teaching such as 6:20-26 or 16:19-31.

Discuss
- What do you think were the nature of John's doubts?

- In terms of hope through Jesus what does it mean when
  you can only experience God's absence?
  you find it difficult to understand?
  you experience a break-up in a relationship?

- What difference does Jesus make in my life?
  How do we go about our main task of helping others receive Jesus as a source of hope?

Exercise
Following on from Luke 7:22
Think of people who might not have hope for the future. e.g people who are homeless, people who are out of work.
Who might be the people who suffer prejudice in our society?

Write beatitudes that challenge our understanding of where hope lies (see Luke 6:20-21).
You could complete the following in your own words.
- Blessed are the poor for they ...
- Blessed are the homeless for they ...
- Blessed are ...

What does this tell us about knowing Jesus Christ today?

Preparation for the next session   5 minutes
The group leader or some other person should collect some stories from newspapers for the next session. The stories need to be examples of events that are both challenging and difficult especially in relation to faith. E.g. How could God let such a tragedy happen to

anyone? Why does the government do this when it hurts so many? What do researchers and doctors think they are up to?

Worship  10 minutes

In this session we have been thinking about hope through Jesus. Read the beatitudes you have written with pauses for thought.

Let us listen carefully to Jesus as he asks us, "who do you say that I am?"

> **Mark 8:27-31**
>
> *27 Jesus went on with his disciples to the villages of Caesarea Philippi; and on the way he asked his disciples, 'Who do people say that I am?' 28 And they answered him, 'John the Baptist; and others, Elijah; and still others, one of the prophets.' 29 He asked them, 'But who do you say that I am?' Peter answered him, 'You are the Messiah.' 30 And he sternly ordered them not to tell anyone about him.*
>
> Pause, to make your own silent response.
>
> *31 Then he began to teach them that the Son of Man must undergo great suffering, and be rejected by the elders, the chief priests, and the scribes, and be killed, and after three days rise again.*

Concluding Prayer
Say together:

We pray for the gift of Hope;
hope for ourselves,
hope for our families, friends, colleagues,
and hope for the world.
We pray that our hope in Jesus
to be people of justice,
companions of the oppressed,

will conquer our fears and doubts
and free us to live the good news about Him,
the one who is to come.
Lord, guide us through this Lenten season,
as we prepare for your resurrection in hope and glory. Amen.

Additional Resources for Session Three

In 79AD the city of Pompeii was destroyed by the eruption of Mount Vesuvius. Less well known is another town, Herculaneum, which suffered in the same way. This town was a popular first century resort until that day Mount Vesuvius exploded and buried it under sixty-five feet of solidified mud and lava.

Herculaneum is interesting in that it was not a wealthy town like Pompeii. Excavations at the site have uncovered blocks of tenements in which the poor lived. The ruins of Herculaneum speak about the lives of ordinary people.

In one old house uncovered in 1938, in a small room on the second floor there was found embedded into a wall panel a small cross. It is an important find because it is among the earliest evidence of the Christian religion in the Roman Empire. The archaeologist saw this cross and knew that a Christian had lived here, a Christian who was very poor, a Christian who was almost isolated from a larger pagan community. Thus this cross was of some interest. The believer saw this cross and began to understand a great deal about this room and its occupants. There was hope in this tiny room, hope in the midst of what must have been a very meagre existence. There was freedom from the Fates that ruled the lives of so many people in ancient days. There was light that comes from the knowledge that one is loved. For in this room lived a Christian, one who believed in Jesus, one who believed that the ultimate meaning of the universe is life-nourishing love. Could anything destroy this hope?

Session 4

Hope Through Tears

Aim
To explore ways in which suffering may contain the seeds of hope for the future.

Welcome and Opening Prayer   5 minutes

Starting point   35 minutes
The leader or someone else will have collected some stories from newspapers. These stories will be examples of events that are difficult and challenging, particularly in relation to faith. Perhaps these may be stories of particular human suffering affecting those such as children who we feel do not 'deserve' this. Take time to share these stories together, allowing people the chance to explain why they find these so problematic. If appropriate also invite members of the group – in twos and threes – to share incidents and events that are personal to them. It is important for this to be a time in which people are allowed freely to express doubts and questions – it will not be helpful if others try and provide 'answers' at this point in the session.

You may also find the following comments by the Methodist minister and theologian Frances Young challenging. She is writing about Arthur, her profoundly handicapped son. In *Face to Face* she looks at what the existence of Arthur and her caring for him has meant for her own faith.

'The phenomenon of handicap can produce a naive sentimentality which refuses to admit it is an evil, but everything in me protested against it as cruel and unnecessary. And if, as I had always been led to believe, every individual is important to God, how could he afflict even one of his creatures in this way, let alone the two per cent of humanity that is born with some handicap or other, denying them the possibility of fullness of life? In terms of traditional Christian views about God's loving purposes I could

make no sense of it.'
(Frances Young, *Face to Face: A Narrative essay in the theology of suffering*, T&T Clark, Edinburgh 1990, p. 58)

How does this passage help us to reflect on the newspapers and stories we have just shared?

Look together at the following comment of John Stott:
'Our groans express both present pain and future longing. Some Christians, however, grin too much (they seem to have no place in their theology for pain) and groan too little.' (John RW Stott from *The Message of Romans*, Bible Speaks Today series, IVP 1994 p.242)

- Does it ring true in your experience?
- Do you feel able to 'groan' – or do you get the impression from Christians that 'groaning' is not allowed?
- How much 'groaning' goes on in your church?

Bible Reading and Discussion   35 minutes

Romans 8:14-27

[14] For all who are led by the Spirit of God are children of God. [15] For you did not receive a spirit of slavery to fall back into fear, but you have received a spirit of adoption. When we cry 'Abba! Father!' [16] it is that very Spirit bearing witness with our spirit that we are children of God, [17] and if children, then heirs, heirs of God and joint heirs with Christ – if, in fact, we suffer with him so that we may also be glorified with him.
[18] I consider that the sufferings of this present time are not worth comparing with the glory about to be revealed to us. [19] For the creation waits with eager longing for the revealing of the children of God; [20] for the creation was subjected to futility, not of its own will but by the will of the one who subjected it, in hope [21] that the creation itself will be set free from its bondage to decay and will obtain the freedom of the glory of the children of God. [22] We know

that the whole creation has been groaning in labour pains until now; ²³ *and not only the creation, but we ourselves, who have the first fruits of the Spirit, groan inwardly while we wait for adoption, the redemption of our bodies.* ²⁴ *For in hope we were saved. Now hope that is seen is not hope. For who hopes for what is seen?* ²⁵ *But if we hope for what we do not see, we wait for it with patience.*
²⁶ *Likewise the Spirit helps us in our weakness; for we do not know how to pray as we ought, but that very Spirit intercedes with sighs too deep for words.* ²⁷ *And God, who searches the heart, knows what is the mind of the Spirit, because the Spirit intercedes for the saints according to the will of God.*

Background To Romans 8:14-27

This isn't an easy passage to read or make sense of today: the letters of Paul rarely are! But it comes at a key point in one of Paul's most important letters, and it touches on so many aspects of the Christian faith – our relationship to God, to Christ, the world, the nature of prayer – so it is worth spending time with it.

- Paul makes assumptions about the common background and world view he shared with his readers. Since we probably don't share so directly these links, we do need to try and think ourselves imaginatively into the position of Paul's readers.

One of the things that Paul shared with those who read his letters was a deep knowledge of the Old Testament. Paul was soaked in and 'breathed' the Old Testament to a degree that few Christians would come close to today. And he assumed that the Christians in Rome did too – even those who were born as Gentiles rather than Jews. After all in Paul's time there wasn't a 'New' Testament – it was the Old Testament alone that was scripture. And just as we try to interpret and make sense of Paul's letters in our modern world, a great deal of Paul's work was trying to make sense of the Old Testament in his world – a world in which Jesus had so recently lived, died and risen again.

So to understand what Paul is saying we need to realise that running like a thread through the whole letter to the Romans is the story of God's creation of the world and of human beings as it is told in the Old Testament book of Genesis. Paul is assuming that we, like his first readers, know that:

- God's Spirit was active in creation of the world at the beginning of time (Genesis 1.2)
- Human beings were created to be God's stewards – helping God with the proper management of creation. (Genesis 1.26-27). One could even use the term 'heir' to picture this role. It seems that Adam could even be called the 'son of God.' (see Luke 3.38)
- Since the word 'Adam' means simply 'human being', it was very easy to draw links between the story of Adam and Eve and the development of the whole human race. That's probably precisely what the writer of Genesis intended us to be doing.
- According to Genesis, Adam and Eve had a particularly close relationship with God. This can be called their 'glory.'
- As a result of human disobedience portrayed in Genesis 3, a number of 'fractures' occurred: fracture in the relationship between human beings and God, between human beings themselves, and in the proper working of creation. All are seen as consequences of that first 'going wrong.' Death was considered to be one of the outcomes of this. In addition the pain of 'labour' is a powerful image used to describe the disruption of such relationships – though it is also significant that such pain can hopefully have a positive outcome.

With this background in mind Paul is seeking to express the

significance of what Jesus Christ had done - for human beings, but also for the world as a whole. Like other early Christians Paul seems to have thought of Jesus as a 'new Adam' – the beginning of a new creation, in which we can all share, where the world would really be as God had always wanted it to be.

Of course Paul was only too aware that the 'old creation' with all its flaws was still very apparent. But if we picture a mechanism that has been moving one way now turned round so that it starts to reverse the process we are beginning to think along Paul's lines. The 'old creation' was being undone, like yeast, the work of Christ was beginning to radically transform the world. It's not an easy, nor a comfortable process, as the new finds itself grating against the old. So the image of 'labour pains' comes to the fore again to describe this. But as John Stott reminded us above, such 'groaning' is not just a statement about the pain of the present but also carries within itself a sense of longing and hope for the future. We hope that 'glory' is to be the eventual destiny of humanity and the created world.

Choose one of the following three topics.

1 Does a faith that God suffers with us provide hope in pain? Look again at the verses from Romans – particularly 8.17. This links our suffering with Christ's suffering. But does God suffer too? And does it help us when we suffer?
For many centuries Christian tradition held strongly to the belief that God could not suffer. God was 'up there,' unchangeable and remote from suffering. Find a copy of the classic hymn 'Immortal, invisible God only wise' and read it through together. It is a very good example of this way of thinking. Then compare some modern hymns, 'Morning glory, starlit sky' and 'I the Lord of sea and sky' are particularly good examples.

'Immortal, invisible God only wise' can be found in many popular hymnals including *Hymns Old and New*, *Celebration Hymnal*, *Hymns and Psalms*, and *Songs of Fellowship*.

'Morning glory, starlit sky' is in *Rejoice and Sing*, and also in *Ancient and Modern New Standard*.

'I the Lord of sea and sky' is in *Hymns Old and New*.

If your own church does not have a copy of one of these hymnals do see if you can borrow one from a neighbouring church.

Here God is pictured not as 'up there' but very much 'down here' and sharing in the powerlessness and pain human beings experience. Do we need both ways of thinking? Which is more true to the Bible? Look at Romans 8.26-27. It comes very close to suggesting that God is groaning in and with and alongside us. Yet if we leave it at this point are we not stopping before the point of hope is reached?

You may find it helpful to reflect on this visually. One way of doing so is by looking at different styles of crosses and crucifixes.

Have available a simple cross, a traditional crucifix in which Christ is portrayed 'hanging' from the cross, a Celtic or other cross. Think about what each of these different symbols is seeking to share with us. Which speaks most powerfully to *you*?

Or 2. Does the experience of women shed special light on the possibility of hope coming through pain?

Within a few days of this meeting many churches will be or will have been celebrating Mothering Sunday. It is also near the moment in the year when some Christians remember Mary's role, in accepting the words of God's messenger that she would be the mother of God's son (March 25, The Feast of the Annunciation). The image of 'labour' that gives birth to the new creation expressed so strongly in our Bible reading (Romans 8.22) is one that speaks to women in a way that goes beyond men's experience. Have women a particular contribution to offer when we think about hope coming through pain?

1998 is also the concluding year of the Decade of Churches in Solidarity with Women. What outcomes, if any, has this Decade had in your church?

Or 3. Does the image of creation 'groaning' have anything to say to us about our role and responsibility towards creation?
With some honourable exceptions, such as St Francis, Christians in history haven't often had a good reputation as far as caring for the world and creation around us is concerned. All too often creation has been viewed primarily from the perspective of human beings. Perhaps we need to think rather more about 'redeeming' and rather less about 'ruling' creation. What are the 'groans' of creation? Can people give examples. Is the fact that these days we are more ready to hear such 'groans' perhaps itself a sign of hope?

Preparation for the next session   5 minutes
In the course of the next week look out for images that you have inspired you. Bring one or two images along with you to the next session if you can.

Worship  10 minutes
In this session we have been thinking about ways in which suffering can lead to hope. In Holy Week we will remember that Jesus suffered, and then rose in glory. This passage from Mark gives us a foretaste of that glory: see it in your mind's eye.

Mark 9:1-9

¹ And he said to them, 'Truly I tell you, there are some standing here who will not taste death until they see that the kingdom of God has come with power.'
² Six days later, Jesus took with him Peter and James and John, and led them up a high mountain apart, by themselves. And he was transfigured before them, ³ and his clothes became dazzling white, such as no one on earth could bleach them. ⁴ And there appeared to

> them Elijah with Moses, who were talking with Jesus. ⁵ Then Peter said to Jesus, 'Rabbi, it is good for us to be here; let us make three dwellings, one for you, one for Moses, and one for Elijah.' ⁶ He did not know what to say, for they were terrified. ⁷ Then a cloud overshadowed them, and from the cloud there came a voice, 'This is my Son, the Beloved; listen to him!' ⁸ Suddenly when they looked around, they saw no one with them any more, but only Jesus.
> ⁹ As they were coming down the mountain, he ordered them to tell no one about what they had seen, until after the Son of Man had risen from the dead.

In a moment of quiet let God speak to you through the symbols in this passage.

There are tears in our world and in ourselves. Let us offer them to God in hope. (pause).

Concluding Prayer
Say together:

Lord of all time,
You reveal to us our fragility,
You uncover in us our treachery.
Renew us and restore us
To walk with you to Golgotha
And keep watch by your side
Until that Easter moment of triumph
When you will overcome our despair
And turn the groaning of your Church
Into a steadfast love,
That we may leave what is past in peace
And embrace the future in hope.
Amen.

Additional Resource for Session 4

The transfiguration of Jesus is one of the most mysterious stories in the New Testament. Its very strangeness has led to it being neglected by many Christians in the west. By contrast among Christians of Eastern Orthodox traditions it has always been cherished and meditated upon. It is a story full of symbolism, the mountain upon which Jesus stands reminds us of the mountain in the Old Testament where God met with Moses. It also seems to recall the Garden of Eden, where God walked with human beings and before the world had become spoiled.

But as well as looking back it looks forward – the image of the 'dwellings' that Peter wishes to build remind us of Revelation's dream that one day God will 'dwell' with human beings and death will be no more. (Revelation 21.3-4). The transfiguration of Jesus sets in train a process whose final goal is to work through the transfiguration of all humanity and which will not be fully complete until the entire cosmos has been renewed, repaired and transfigured. But the story of the transfiguration does not end on the mountain-top - neither for Jesus nor for us. Its real meaning cannot be understood without coming down to the valley. It is a glory which cannot come to fruition without the journey to Jerusalem, without the suffering on the cross, without dying, death, and resurrection. It is a hope which can only happen when and if the presence of pain is accepted, allowed and redeemed.

Session 5

Hope Through Vision

Aim
To reflect on the course and show how hope can be inspired by imaginative visions.

Welcome and Opening Prayer   5 minutes

Starting Point   15 minutes
The session leader reminds group members of the journey made in the previous four sessions. In preparation for this session, members were asked to be on the look-out for images which have inspired them in the course of the week. Take a few minutes to exchange impressions with another group member.

Bible Reading and Discussion   45 minutes
The reason for this attention to images is because the text for today is full of them. The Revelation to John (sometimes called The Book of the Apocalypse) invites us into the awesome wonder of God's loving purpose, the basis of all our hope. It was written some seventy years after Jesus died, rose, ascended and sent the Holy Spirit. There was persecution; the good news did not seem to be getting through. The followers of Jesus needed to remember it was God's work they were doing!

One way of reading God's Word is to go with its flow rather than to fight it. Let the Spirit of God work on us through the images in the text. Treated in this way, the text becomes a prayer rather than a study. There are no 'right' answers: different things will strike different people at different times, in the light of their own experience. Be as comfortable as you can and don't be hurried. This is the Word of the Lord in dramatic and poetic form. An angel is showing the writer around the City of God, as though in a dream. Let's savour and relish this vision, thinking about where we see the images of hope here?

Revelation 21:23 - 22:5

²³ *The city has no need of sun or moon to shine on it, for the glory of God is its light, and its light is the Lamb.* ²⁴ *The nations will walk by its light, and the kings of the earth will bring their glory into it.* ²⁵ *Its gates will never be shut by day - and there will be no night there.* ²⁶ *People will bring into it the glory and the honour of the nations.* ²⁷ *But nothing unclean will enter it, nor anyone who practises abomination or falsehood, but only those who are written in the Lamb's book of life.*

¹ *Then the angel showed me the river of the water of life, bright as crystal, flowing from the throne of God and of the Lamb* ² *through the middle of the street of the city. On either side of the river is the tree of life, with its twelve kinds of fruit, producing its fruit each month; and the leaves of the tree are for the healing of the nations.* ³ *Nothing accursed will be found there any more. But the throne of God and of the Lamb will be in it, and his servants will worship him;* ⁴ *they will see his face, and his name will be on their foreheads.* ⁵ *And there will be no more night; they need no light of lamp or sun, for the Lord God will be their light, and they will reign forever and ever.*

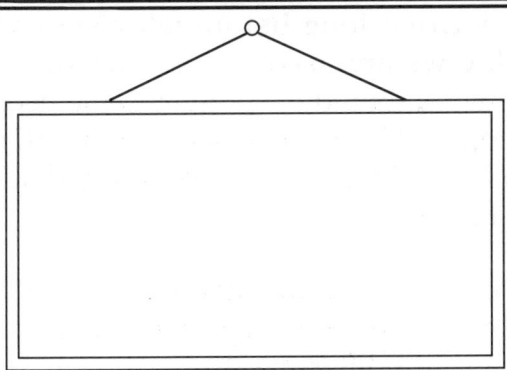

Here is a picture frame: the picture (image) itself is in your head now, after that reading. Jot it down before it slips away. (Is it hopeful?)

Reflecting

> It is easy to see that we are dealing here with a kind of writing which is foreign to our culture today. 'The Lamb' is familiar as an image of Jesus – do you remember John the Baptist's words? The emphasis on light and dark is not as striking for most of us now as it was in the days before electricity was harnessed and street lights invented! The reference to rivers flowing through the town has to be understood in the context of a desert country where such abundance could only be dreamt about. Thrones are spoken of as signs of authority. And did you notice the reference to natural medicines?

When you feel ready, take up one or some of the following suggestions, as time allows. The idea is not to finish everything but rather to see our own experience in the light of God's word, and God's word in the light of our lived experience.

In twos or threes first of all, discuss – what hope and what images of hope did this passage give you?

Our text was written long before television and video were invented. Today we are used to cascades of images from the media. What images should we present to the people around here to offer them hope? (Have you a picture in mind?)
In this time of Lent, Christians reflect on the shadow of the cross in the light of Easter.

- When do we find it hard to witness to our faith in Jesus? How could we do a better job of it around here? (Should the Millennium make a difference?)
- Who do you think are the real servants of God, the people of God's hope, today? How can we join them? (If some of these are not Church-goers, where does that leave those of us who are?)

- Refreshing streams and fruitful trees: how can we bring new heart to our neighbours' lives – and our own? What would we like to see put on a 'tree of life'?

Re-Reading
Now that we have explored the text, let's read it through slowly again and see what strikes us particularly this time.

Deciding
Following this Lent course what one practical thing can we agree to do which will make a difference – however small? (Let's not promise more than we can deliver!)

Evaluating   15 minutes
In a moment of quiet, weigh up your feelings about these Lent '98 sessions.
What, for me, was good about them?
What, for me, was difficult about them?
What, for me, will be the most important effect on the way I live my life?
What suggestion would I give to make future Lent programmes even better?

Arrange for one member of the group to fill out the evaluation form at the back of this book.

Worship    10 minutes
It only remains now to bring our group's work, fellowship and concerns to the loving God of Hope. In Mark's gospel, the last story before Jesus enters Jerusalem for Holy Week is that of his meeting with the blind man, Bartimaeus. His story is full of images which may help us: even poor beggars like us can be given clear sight and become true disciples! Let God talk to us through this story – and let us be thankful for the hope the Father gives us in the Son and the Spirit.

> **Mark 10: 46-52**
> ⁴⁶ ... *As he and his disciples and a large crowd were leaving Jericho, Bartimaeus son of Timaeus, a blind beggar, was sitting by the roadside.* ⁴⁷ *When he heard that it was Jesus of Nazareth, he began to shout out and say, 'Jesus, Son of David, have mercy on me!'*
> ⁴⁸ *Many sternly ordered him to be quiet, but he cried out even more loudly, 'Son of David, have mercy on me!'*
> ⁴⁹ *Jesus stood still and said, 'Call him here'. And they called the blind man, saying to him, 'Take heart; get up, he is calling you.'*
> ⁵⁰ *So throwing off his cloak, he sprang up and came to Jesus.*
> ⁵¹ *Then Jesus said to him, 'What do you want me to do for you?' The blind man said to him, 'My teacher, let me see again.'* ⁵² *Jesus said to him, 'Go; your faith has made you well.' Immediately he regained his sight and followed him on the way.*

Let's thank God for the things he has shown us in these sessions, in our lives, in our world.
(The group members may have prayers to voice or to carry in their hearts.)

Concluding Prayer
Say together:

Lord God,
enable us to see your visions
and to dream your dreams.
Bless all who work for your kingdom.
Give us the heart and strength this Holy Week
to spring up and come to Jesus
like Bartimaeus did.
We thank you for bringing us together:
keep us united in your Spirit of love.
We ask this through Jesus Christ, our Lord. Amen.

May the grace of our Lord Jesus Christ, the love of God, and the fellowship of the Holy Spirit, be with us all evermore, Amen.

Useful Addresses

Further resources and information:

CCBI Bookroom, Inter-Church House, 35-41 Lower Marsh, London SE1 7RL.

Partners in Learning Distribution, 1020 Bristol Road, Selly Oak, Birmingham B29 6LB.

Community of Women and Men in the Church, Inter-Church House, 35-41 Lower Marsh, London SE1 7RL.

Jubilee 2000, PO Box 100, London SE1 7RT.

The Open Book, c/o Bible Society, Stonehill Green, Westlea, Swindon SN5 7DG

Copies of the CTE Millennium booklet can be ordered from: Church House Bookshop, 31 Great Smith Street, London SW1P 3BN

Ecumenical Bodies in Britain and Ireland

Action of Churches Together in Scotland (ACTS), Scottish Churches House, Dunblane FK15 0AJ

Churches Together in England, Inter-Church House, 35-41 Lower Marsh, London SE1 7RL.

CYTUN (Churches Together in Wales), 11 St Helen's Road, Swansea SA1 4AL

The Irish Council of Churches, Inter-Church Centre, 46 Elmwood Avenue, Belfast BT9 6AZ

The Council of Churches for Britain and Ireland, Inter-Church House, 35-41 Lower Marsh, London SE1 7RL.

Members of the Lent 1998 Planning Group

Donald Elliott	Churches Commission on Mission (Moderator)
Colin Brady	Churches Together in South Yorkshire (Co-ordinator)
Clare Amos	Partners in Learning
Jeff Bonser	Churches Advisory Council on Local Broadcasting
Aled Davies	CYTUN (Churches Together in Wales)
Christine Dodd	Roman Catholic Church
Colin Garley	Churches Together in England
Maggie Hindley	United Reformed Church
Walter Houston	Consultant
Pauline Huggan	Black Christian Concerns Group
Judy Jarvis	Consultative Group on Ministry Among Children
Tony McCaffry	Christian Adult Learning Meeting
David Rudiger	CCBI Publications
Maureen Slattery	ACTS (Action of Churches Together in Scotland)
Colin Davey	CCBI (Editor)

Evaluation

Hope in a Time of Change is the Lent Course published by the Council of Churches for Britain and Ireland for use in 1998. The course will be used by many churches and local groups and is the latest in the series of courses published every two years. (*Have Another Look* was the CCBI course in 1994 and *Building Bridges* was the course in 1996).

Your comments on the experience of this course will help in the preparation of future courses. Please send your comments to: Lent 98 Evaluation, CCBI, Inter-Church House, 35-41 Lower Marsh, London SE1 7RL by 8th May 1998 at the latest.

In the first six questions where the statement is followed by numbers 1-4 please circle:
1   if you strongly agree with the statement
2   if you agree with the statement
3   if you disagree with the statement
4   if you strongly disagree with the statement

1   Theme

The theme was challenging	1	2	3	4
The focus on five different aspects of the theme was helpful	1	2	3	4

2   Bible passages

| The passages were stimulating | 1 | 2 | 3 | 4 |
| The discussion of the passages was helpful and exciting | 1 | 2 | 3 | 4 |

3   Background to Bible passages

| The background information was helpful | 1 | 2 | 3 | 4 |
| The background information presented new knowledge | 1 | 2 | 3 | 4 |

4   Discussion

| I found the discussion interesting | 1 | 2 | 3 | 4 |
| Our group got into discussion easily | 1 | 2 | 3 | 4 |

5   Worship

| I appreciated the time of worship and prayer | 1 | 2 | 3 | 4 |
| The passages from the Gospel of St Mark helped us to reflect on the sessions | 1 | 2 | 3 | 4 |

6   The Sessions

| The sessions took too long | 1 | 2 | 3 | 4 |
| The five sessions developed the theme of hope in a time of change | 1 | 2 | 3 | 4 |

7   Have you ever done a Lent Course before?   Yes / No

    If Yes, how did this course compare?

8   Which session did you find most interesting?
    Which session did you find least interesting?

9   Think back over each of the five sessions. Have you any particular comments about any of them? You might find questions 1-6 above helpful in thinking about how the sessions worked.

    Please use an extra sheet of paper if your comments won't fit into the spaces provided.

10 Our group rated the course as a whole (please circle one number)

    1   Very good   2   Good   3   Acceptable   4   Poor

11 Did the course help you find reasons for hope?   Yes / No
    Please say why / in what ways

12 Please use the following space to write any other comments or suggestions you would like to make to the planning group.

13 Identify one thing to do with hope in a time of change which you would like to share with those going from churches in Britain and Ireland to the eighth WCC Assembly at Harare in December 1998 on the theme 'Turn to God: Rejoice in Hope'.

14 **For group leaders**
    Was this an easy course to lead? Please say why you thought this.

    Have you any suggestions for other group leaders?